THE BEST OF

CHEFCLUB RECIPES TO SHARE

THE BEST OF

CHEFCLUB RECIPES TO SHARE

CHEFCLUB

PUBLISHING

2018, Snacking Media
53, rue de Chabrol
75010 Paris - France

All rights of translation, adaptation and reproduction, total or partial, for any use,
by any means whatsoever, reserved for all countries.

Legal deposit: June 2018
ISBN: 978-2-490129-09-6
Printed in Italy by Print Co in June 2018

The brands mentioned in the book are not advertising and are only the choice of the publisher.
Coca-Cola®, Doritos®, M&M's®, Nutella®, Kinder®, Sprite®, Tabasco® and Ziploc® are registered trademarks.

Alcohol abuse is dangerous for your health, consume in moderation.

CONTENTS

INTRODUCTION

When the ingredients of our cupboards become the big stars of small screens—phones, tablets, computers—Chefclub gourmet feasts are all over the world!

You are now part of more than 30 million suscribers from all over the world who follow our recipe videos. We are very proud of our small team of 25 people from France, Italy, Brazil, Germany, the UK, and more. While we satisfy our own cravings every day (as you can probably imagine!), we also work hard and each of your comments or shares encourages us in our culinary adventures. We therefore wanted to first and foremost thank you from the bottom of our hearts for your commitment to us.

Chefclub seeks to transform the kitchen into a space for sharing food and fun.

The videos—and now our first book!—are there to guide, inspire, amuse, but above all share, and the sections of the book are organized with this principle in mind.
The first part, *Family*, is dedicated to simple and delicious recipes that will have the whole family gathered round the table in the blink of an eye!
The second part, *Friends*, includes recipes for appetizers and are designed for sharing among friends.
The third part, *Love*, is made up of slightly more elaborate recipes that require careful attention… the same level of attention usually reserved for your other half.
The fourth part, the *Bonus* section is a gift! Have your cake and eat it too!

Consume in moderation…

Happy reading and bon appétit!

The Chefclub team

45

RECIPES TO SHARE

It's reeeeeaaaaady!

FAMILY

LASAGNA SANDWICH

LASAGNA YOU CAN TAKE ANYWHERE!

 3 PEOPLE

 PREPARATION
15 minutes

 INGREDIENTS

For 3 lasagna paninis:
6 slices of white bread
3 ½ tbsp butter
6 pieces of cooked lasagna
1 carrot
1 onion
1 cup ground beef
3.5 oz red wine
⅔ cup tomato sauce
1 ⅓ cups bechamel sauce
1 ½ cups grated mozzarella
Olive oil

 EQUIPMENT
1 panini press
1 frying pan

1 Spread the melted butter onto one side of the slices of bread, then turn 3 pieces over and place a sheet of cooked lasagna on each one.

2 Brown the ground beef, carrot, and onion in a frying pan with a drizzle of olive oil (1). Add the red wine and tomato sauce and mix together (2).

3 Add 1 tablespoon of the meat mixture onto the lasagna sheet, cover with a second pasta sheet and then add 1 tablespoon of bechamel. Cover with a third sheet of lasagna.

4 Sprinkle with grated mozzarella and close each sandwich with the remaining 3 slices of bread, with the buttered sides facing out (3).

5 Cook the lasagna sandwiches in a panini press for 3 minutes, then serve with a side of salad (4).

 CHEFCLUB TIP
If you don't have a panini press you can make these in a frying pan instead! Use a spatula to press down on the sandwich in the frying pan to get a nice crispy outside, and flip it carefully to make sure none of the filling falls out!

STUFFED PASTA CROWN

A FLOWER OF PASTA! ROMANCE IN THE KITCHEN

 4 PEOPLE

 PREPARATION
40 minutes

 INGREDIENTS
15 oz jumbo pasta shells
18 oz ricotta
7 oz ham
¾ cup grated parmesan
¾ cup grated mozzarella
1 ⅓ cups bechamel sauce
½ bunch of parsley
Salt and pepper

 EQUIPMENT
1 large pie plate

1 Cook the pasta for 12 minutes in a large pot of salted boiling water until they are al dente.

2 Cut the ham into slices and mix in a bowl with the ricotta, parmesan, chopped parsley, salt and pepper (1). Stuff the pasta shells with this mixture (2).

3 Spread the bechamel sauce over the bottom of the pie dish and arrange the pasta like flower petals on the bechamel (3). Sprinkle the grated mozzarella between the pasta shells.

4 Bake for 20 minutes at 375°F. Let it cool slightly before eating, by picking out the pasta shells one by one (4).

 CHEFCLUB TIP
The secret is to avoid overcooking the pasta so it can be handled. To do this, once the shells have finished cooking, drain and plunge them immediately in water filled with ice cubes! This will keep them from cooking any longer.

PIZZA FLAMBÉ

FIRE UP THE PIZZA!

 4 PEOPLE

 PREPARATION
20 minutes

 INGREDIENTS
2 ready-to-bake pizza doughs
⅓ cup tomato sauce
1 large buffalo mozzarella ball
4 slices of ham
10 black olives
3 oz rum
1 ½ cups arugula
Oregano
Balsamic vinegar
Olive oil

 EQUIPMENT
4 straws

1 On the first pizza dough, spread the tomato sauce and add slices of mozzarella and black olives. Sprinkle with oregano (1).

2 Using a brush, paint water around the edge of the dough. Place the straws on the edge (2) and cover the pizza with the second piece of pizza dough. Fold the edges of the 2 doughs together tightly to make a seal (3-4). Blow into the straws to make the dough swell up (5) then remove the straws and quickly seal the edges of the dough together to maintain the air pocket.

3 Bake for 12 minutes at 400°F. When finished, pour the hot rum onto the pizza and light with a match (6).

4 Use scissors to cut open the pizza dome (7). Garnish the pizza with arugula leaves and ham (8). Use the dome as a salad bowl, filling it with arugula and seasoning with olive oil and balsamic vinegar, then enjoy (9).

 CHEFCLUB TIP
The best pizza has a crispy dough. If you want to get as close as possible to the real "pizza oven" effect, and have spare roof tiles in your garage, preheat your oven to the maximum temperature with the tiles inside. Then cook your pizza on the tiles at the specified time and temperature. You'll see the difference!

MEDITERRANEAN PASTRY CROWN

BRING THE TASTES OF ITALY TO YOUR TABLE WITH THIS SIMPLE PASTRY TART

 4 PEOPLE

 PREPARATION
30 minutes

 INGREDIENTS
1 tomato
1 zucchini
1 puff pastry sheet
⅓ cup pesto
9 mini buffalo mozzarella balls
⅓ cup feta cheese
1 egg
5 black olives
Oregano

 EQUIPMENT
1 small bowl
1 baking tray

1 Unroll the puff pastry, place a bowl in the center, and spread the pesto on the pastry in a ring around the bowl.

2 Cut the tomato and zucchini into thick slices and layer alternately on top of the pesto (1). Add the mini mozzarella balls and feta onto the vegetables and top with a sprinkle of dried oregano.

3 Remove the bowl from the midde and cut a star in the middle of the pastry with a knife (2). Gently fold the outer edge of the pastry inwards, and the pastry star pieces over the top of the vegetables and cheese (3).

4 Brush the pastry with egg yolk and add slices of olives on top of the pastry star triangles. Bake for 20 minutes at 375°F and enjoy warm with salad on the side (4).

 CHEFCLUB TIP
Don't have pesto handy? Don't worry, you can easily make it! Mix about 1 cup of fresh basil leaves in a blender with a pinch of salt, 1 tbsp of toasted pine nuts, ⅓ cup of grated parmesan, ½ a garlic clove and a drizzle of olive oil. You can add more or less olive oil to change the consistency of the pesto to suit your taste. Give it a try!

TWICE-BAKED POTATOES

MELTY AND DELICIOUS

 4 PEOPLE

 PREPARATION
40 minutes

 INGREDIENTS
½ cup diced bacon
4 tbsp of crème fraîche
4 eggs
⅓ cup grated mozzarella
Parsley
Salt and pepper

 EQUIPMENT
1 baking sheet
Baking paper

1 Cook the potatoes for 20 minutes in salted boiling water, then take them out and remove the middle of the potato with a spoon.

2 Fry the bacon in the pan. Spread a layer of the crème fraîche in the bottom of each potato skin and add the cooked bacon on top. Crack an egg into each potato and sprinkle grated mozzarella on the egg white.

3 Bake for 15 minutes at 350°F. After baking, sprinkle with salt and pepper and garnish with chopped parsley before serving.

 CHEFCLUB TIP
To save time, you can cook the potatoes in the microwave! Prick them with a fork and microwave for about 10 minutes on full power.

BACON-WRAPPED LASAGNA

A CRISPY WRAPPER FOR DELICIOUS LASAGNA

 6 PEOPLE

 PREPARATION
45 minutes

 INGREDIENTS
8 oz lasagna sheets
1 cup ground beef
1 cup tomato sauce
2 cups bechamel sauce
30 slices of bacon
1 ½ cups grated mozzarella
1 onion
Mixed herbs

 EQUIPMENT
1 loaf pan

1 Cook the beef and chopped onion together in a frying pan, then add the tomato sauce and mixed herbs (1). Simmer for a few minutes, stirring the mixture regularly.

2 Fully cover the base and sides of the loaf pan with the bacon slices, placing the bacon slices perpendicular to the walls of the pan (2).

3 Place a layer of lasagna sheets on the bacon in the bottom of the pan (3). Add a layer of bechamel (4), a layer of grated mozzarella, and a layer of the bolognaise sauce on top (5). Repeat the layers to fill the entire pan and finish with a layer of bechamel and grated mozzarella.

4 Fold the ends of the bacon slices over the mozzarella to close the 'loaf' (6-7), and bake for 45 minutes at 350°F (8). Once baked, remove from the pan and enjoy hot (9).

 CHEFCLUB TIP
For a delicious variant on this recipe, use a peeler to slice different vegetables (such as carrots, eggplant, and zucchini) and substitute them for the bacon.

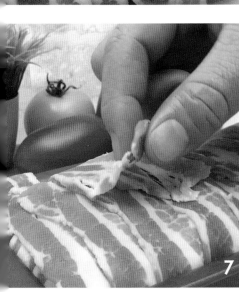

VEGETABLE FLOWER TART

AN EDIBLE BUNCH OF FLOWERS, PERFECT FOR A SUMMER'S DAY

 6 PEOPLE

 PREPARATION
50 minutes

 INGREDIENTS
1 shortcrust pastry sheet
1 green zucchini
1 yellow zucchini
1 carrot
1 eggplant
1 large buffalo mozzarella ball
2 eggs
⅔ cups cream
1 tbsp mustard
Salt and pepper

 EQUIPMENT
1 large pie dish
1 peeler
Baking paper

1 Cut the zucchinis, the carrot and the eggplant into thin and even slices using a peeler.

2 Place the pastry in the bottom of the pie dish. Spread the mustard over the pastry on the bottom of the dish, then add slices of mozzarella.

3 Roll all the vegetable strips up into tight rolls and place them upright in the pie dish. In a bowl, combine the eggs, cream, salt and pepper, and pour the mixture over the vegetable rolls.

4 Bake for 35 minutes at 350°F, then enjoy the vegetable flower tart hot with a salad on the side.

 CHEFCLUB TIP
This recipe is ideal for any leftover vegetables at the bottom of your fridge. To freshen wilted veggies, soak them in water with vinegar and two small spoonfuls of sugar. This lends a second life to our friends from the garden!

RAINBOW TART

A BEAUTIFUL DISPLAY OF COLOR THAT TASTES AS GOOD AS IT LOOKS

 4 PEOPLE

 PREPARATION
50 minutes

 INGREDIENTS
2 sheets of puff pastry
1 green pepper
1 yellow pepper
1 red pepper
1 orange pepper
1 large buffalo mozzarella ball
4 slices of ham
1 egg
Salt and pepper

 EQUIPMENT
1 baking tray
Baking paper
Ruler
Pastry brush

1 To prepare the base:
Cut a square as large as possible in the first sheet of puff pastry, then brush the edges of the square with beaten egg (1). Place the slices of ham and slices of mozzarella in the center then sprinkle with salt and pepper (2).

2 To prepare the checkerboard top:
Cut another large square in the second sheet of puff pastry, and cut it all into ¾"-wide strips. Position one strip vertically over the ends of the others on the left of the square (3). Fold the top strip back over the vertical strip of pastry, then do the same for every other strip (4). To finish, cut the peppers into half-inch strips (5).

3 To prepare the grid:
Arrange a strip of pepper of the same color in a line alongside the vertical pastry strip, then cover over with the folded-back strips of pastry (6). Fold the second set of pastry strips back to the left and place another line of pepper strips of another color. Repeat the process alternating the peppers and strips to form a checkerboard (7). Arrange the remaining 3 strips of pastry on the outside frame to create a border around it.

4 Place the checkerboard sheet onto the base (8) and press lightly so that the egg makes the dough stick together. Paint beaten egg over the tart with a brush. Bake for 30 minutes at 400°F and enjoy hot (9).

 CHEFCLUB TIP
If you don't have a ruler handy to make the strips of pastry, use the cardboard packaging from the pastry to get straight edges. Also remember, the more bands of pepper and pastry you do, the more impressive the result will be!

CANNELLONI CAKE

SHHH...DON'T TELL OUR ITALIAN FRIENDS!

4 PEOPLE

PREPARATION
35 minutes

INGREDIENTS
1 box (250 g) cannelloni pasta
1 ¾ cups ground beef
1 red onion
2 garlic cloves
1 ½ cups tomato sauce
¾ cup grated parmesan
1 large buffalo mozzarella ball
Rosemary
Basil

EQUIPMENT
1 springform pan

1 Brown the beef with the minced onion and garlic in a frying pan with a drizzle of olive oil (1). Add a pinch of rosemary and the tomato sauce and let cook for 10 minutes (2), then cover the bottom of a round baking pan with a layer of beef (3).

2 Cook the cannelloni for 3 minutes in boiling salted water (4), then drain and place them upright in the baking pan (5). Stuff each cannelloni with beef and sprinkle parmesan cheese on top (6-7).

3 Cut the mozzarella into slices and place on top (8). Cook for 15 minutes at 400°F. Allow to cool for several minutes, then serve the pasta with basil leaves (9). Enjoy hot.

CHEFCLUB TIP
For stress-free and catastrophe-free serving, a springform pan is ideal! It guarantees beautiful servings and a mess-free cleanup.

QUICK QUICHE

QUICK AND READY TO GO ANYTIME!

 4 PEOPLE

 PREPARATION
30 minutes

 INGREDIENTS
4 slices of bread
6 eggs
2 slices of ham
⅔ cups grated cheddar
⅔ cups grated mozzarella
1 red pepper
1 onion
1 bunch of chives
Salt and pepper

 EQUIPMENT
1 square baking tin
2 pieces baking paper

1 Lay the pieces of baking paper across each other in the baking tin, and place the slices of bread with crusts removed (1) at the bottom.

2 Beat the eggs in a bowl, and season with salt and pepper. Stir in diced pepper, chopped onion, chopped ham, chopped chives, and both grated cheeses (2). Pour the mix into the baking tin (3).

3 Bake for 20 minutes at 350°F. After baking, cut the quiche into 8 triangles (4). Enjoy hot either at home or on the go—it's up to you!

 CHEFCLUB TIP
You can make this quiche even more light and fluffy! Beat the egg whites first, then add the beaten yolks and gently stir in the rest of the mixture, then cover the slices of bread. You'll get XXL sandwiches with the same amount of ingredients!

ZIPLOC ® OMELETTE

THE EASY NO-FUSS SOLUTION TO PREVENT SCRAMBLED EGGS

 2 PEOPLE

 PREPARATION
20 minutes

 INGREDIENTS
6 eggs
1 slice of ham
½ red pepper
½ green pepper
1 onion
¾ cups grated mozzarella
¾ cups grated cheddar
½ avocado
Tomato sauce
Salt and pepper

 EQUIPMENT
1 large saucepan
1 Ziploc bag®

1 Cut the peppers into small cubes, cut the ham into thin slices, and finely chop the onion.

2 Crack the eggs into the Ziploc® bag and season with salt and pepper. Close the bag and shake vigorously! Open the bag and add the onion, peppers, ham and grated cheese (1). Close the bag and shake again to mix the ingredients together.

3 Immerse the bag in the pan of simmering water (2) and cook for 15 minutes. Remove the omelette from the bag (3) and enjoy with tomato sauce and avocado on the side (4).

 CHEFCLUB TIP
In order to get an evenly cooked omelette, avoid putting the Ziploc® bag into direct contact with the pan. To do this, you can hold the bag in the water by piercing the top of the bag and holding it with a pair of chopsticks resting on the edge of the pan.

LIL' BREAKFAST ROLL

...BREAKFAST FOR EVERY MEAL OF THE DAY!

 4 PEOPLE

 PREPARATION
20 minutes

 INGREDIENTS
4 bread rolls
3 ½ oz bacon
4 eggs
¾ cups crème fraîche
⅓ cup grated mozzarella
2 tsp butter
Parsley
Salt and pepper

 EQUIPMENT
1 baking tray
Baking paper

1 Cut the top off of the bread rolls and remove the bread from the middle. Butter the bread roll tops then cut them into breadsticks.

2 Spread a layer of crème fraîche onto the bottom of the rolls. Fry the bacon then place it inside the rolls. Add grated mozzarella then break an egg into each roll.

3 Put the rolls and the bread sticks into the oven for 10 minutes at 350°F on a baking tray. Remove the rolls from the oven, season with salt and pepper and sprinkle with chopped parsley. Enjoy by dipping the toasted breadsticks into the cheesy, egg-filled bread roll center.

 CHEFCLUB TIP
To cook the bacon quickly, simply wrap it in paper towels and place in a microwaveable container for about 2 minutes. The bacon will be perfectly cooked, and the grease will be soaked into the paper towel instead of on the bacon.

TOMATO & MOZZARELLA 3 WAYS

ENJOY 3 DIFFERENT VERSIONS OF THIS CLASSIC COMBINATION

 6 PEOPLE

 PREPARATION
60 minutes

 INGREDIENTS
10 slices of bread
2 tomatoes
3 large buffalo mozzarella balls
3 tbsp green pesto
375 ml white wine
7 oz mini buffalo mozzarella balls
7 oz cherry tomatoes
1 garlic clove
Basil
Thyme
1 slice of parma ham
2 eggs
1 cup flour
1 ⅔ cups breadcrumbs
2 cups vegetable oil
Olive oil
Salt and pepper

 EQUIPMENT
1 toaster
1 baking tray
Aluminum foil
Baking paper
Skewers

1 Sandwich:
On a square of aluminium foil (12"x12") place a slightly smaller square of baking paper. Brush one side of a piece of bread with olive oil and place it on the paper oil side down. Cover the other side of the bread with a layer of pesto, 2 slices of tomato, and 2 slices of mozzarella. Finish with a few extra dollops of pesto (1), then add a second slice of bread on top, and brush the top with more olive oil (2). Close the foil around the sandwich by wrapping up 3 sides, and cook for 4 minutes at full power in the microwave (3).

2 Fondue:
Melt the small mozzarella balls in a saucepan with the white wine, and season with salt and pepper (4). Cut the bread into crouton-size cubes and brush them with a mix of the chopped garlic, thyme and olive oil. Bake for 5 minutes at 180°C (5). Make skewers of a cherry tomato, a basil leaf and the toasted crouton then dip them in the fondue (6).

3 Croquette:
Cut the top of the large mozzarella balls to create a hat, leaving one edge still attached. Hollow out the middles and stuff them with chopped tomato, half a slice of parma ham and a basil leaf (7). Coat the balls in flour, beaten egg and breadcrumbs and fry them for 4 minutes in hot oil. Enjoy all your creations! (8-9)

 CHEFCLUB TIP
To choose the right tomato: if it is soft and the stem falls off at first touch be careful, then it is too ripe...and if it has a thin skin, it was grown in a greenhouse.

CAULIFLOWER PIZZA

BUSTING THE MYTH THAT GLUTEN-FREE IS TASTE-FREE!

 4 PEOPLE

 PREPARATION
35 minutes

 INGREDIENTS
1 cauliflower
1 tsp corn flour
3 eggs
1 cup tomato sauce
3 slices of ham
1 large buffalo mozzarella ball
12 black olives
Oregano
Basil
Parsley
Salt and pepper

 EQUIPMENT
1 baking tray
Baking paper

1 Chop the cauliflower into very fine pieces, then add the eggs, salt, pepper, and chopped parsley and mix well (1). On a baking tray lined with baking paper, spread the mixture into a disk shape and bake for 10 minutes at 350°F.

2 Once cooked, add a layer of tomato sauce to your cauliflower pizza base (2). Then add a pinch of oregano, the ham, sliced mozzarella, and black olives (3).

3 Bake in the oven for 15 minutes at 400°F. Garnish with fresh basil leaves and serve hot (4).

 CHEFCLUB TIP
Cauliflower makes a great gluten-free alternative for bread and pasta. You can make cauliflower rice or couscous by frying finely chopped cauliflower with a tablespoon of water for 5 minutes in a frying pan, or mix with egg and cheese and fry for 5 minutes each side to make an alternative slice of toast. It's low-fat and low-carb too, so it's a great option for anyone trying to lose weight!

HOT DOG TART

A NEW WAY TO EAT YOUR HOT DOGS

4 PEOPLE

PREPARATION

30 minutes

INGREDIENTS

2 sheets puff pastry
1 cup mozzarella
8 hot dogs
1 onion
1 egg yolk
¾ cups vegetable oil
Mustard
Ketchup

EQUIPMENT

1 baking tray
Baking paper

1 Cut the mozzarella cheese into slices and then into thin strips. Make a lengthwise cut in the hot dogs, and stuff the mozzarella strips into the cuts.

2 Cut the pastry into a rectangle the same width as the full length of the hot dogs. Cut the rectangle into 5 strips, leaving the left side edge of the pastry uncut to hold it all together. Form a checkerboard of pastry and hot dog by alternating the hot dogs and strips of pastry, following the same process as the rainbow pie on page 26.

3 Cut the onion into rings, and fry for 3-4 minutes in hot oil. Cut the second puff pastry sheet to the same width as the checkerboard, but slightly longer. Put the fried onion onto the second pastry sheet.

4 Put the checkerboard pastry sheet on top of the onion and fold the edges of the bottom sheet of pastry over to make the edges. Brush the pastry with egg yolk.

5 Bake for 15 minutes at 400°F, then decorate with mustard and ketchup and serve with a side of salad.

CHEFCLUB TIP

To make the original fried onion recipe, it's just as simple but requires a little more patience. Dip the onions in a mixture of milk, salt and paprika, coat them in flour and fry until brown.

Nothing beats breaking bread with friends!

FRIENDS

CARBONARA CROWN

THE ULTIMATE CHEESY PASTA-FONDUE FUSION

 6 PEOPLE

 PREPARATION
35 minutes

 INGREDIENTS
9 oz spaghetti
1 wheel camembert cheese
7 oz diced bacon
¾ cups grated parmesan
4 eggs
Cherry tomatoes
Basil

 EQUIPMENT
1 round cake tin

1 Cook the spaghetti for 8 minutes in a large saucepan of salted boiling water, then drain.

2 Fry the bacon in the saucepan and add the cooked spaghetti, eggs, and parmesan cheese. Mix everything together well (1).

3 Place the camembert wheel, still inside its wooden box, into the center of the round cake tin with the wooden lid removed. Place the spaghetti mix all around the camembert (2).

4 Bake for 20 minutes at 400°F. After cooking, remove the lid of the cheese (3) and garnish the crown with a few basil leaves and cherry tomatoes (4). Eat by dipping chunks of the pasta crown into the cheesy fondue.

 CHEFCLUB TIP
To make the pasta even crispier, you can pan fry it. Pour the pasta mix into an oiled pan and cook without stirring the mixture. When it starts to stick together, use a lid to flip the pasta over and cook the other side for a few more minutes.

CHEESE FONDUE DIPPERS

ALL-IN-ONE CHEESE FONDUE READY TO SERVE AND ENJOY

 6 PEOPLE

 PREPARATION
25 minutes

 INGREDIENTS
2 puff pastry sheets
10 hot dogs
1 wheel of brie
2 cups sundried tomatoes
1 egg yolk
1 garlic clove
Chives

 EQUIPMENT
1 baking tray
Baking paper

1 Using a knife, cut a circle out of the top of the brie and remove the rind lid. Add chopped sundried tomatoes, finely chopped garlic and chopped chives into the top of the brie (1).

2 Put the rind lid back on the top of the brie (2) and place it in the middle of a circular puff pastry sheet. Arrange 5 hot dogs around the brie, and fold the pastry edges over the top of the hot dogs, then cut each hot dog sausage into fifths (3-5).

3 Lift and rotate each hot dog piece 90° (6). On the second sheet of puff pastry, cut pastry strips the size of the hot dogs and wrap them in the pastry, then cut them into fifths again.

4 Place the wrapped hot dogs in a layer on top of the previous ones to create a double layer around the brie (7), then brush with egg yolk.

5 Bake for 20 minutes at 400°F on a baking tray. Once cooked, remove the lid from the brie and dip the hot dogs into the cheese fondue (8-9).

 CHEFCLUB TIP
For this recipe, you can make it even more gourmet by adding a little white wine. Pour 1.5 oz of wine inside the brie with the sundried tomatoes, garlic and chives before cooking, then enjoy your amazing creation!

MEATBALL LOLLIPOPS

A SNACK, A STARTER OR A PICNIC? THIS RECIPE IS YOUR GO-TO CROWD PLEASER!

 3 PEOPLE

 PREPARATION
40 minutes

 INGREDIENTS
For 6 lollipops:
1 cup ground beef
6 mini buffalo mozzarella balls
6 small onions
12 slices of bacon
1 egg
Barbecue sauce
Salt and pepper
Parsley

 EQUIPMENT
1 baking tray
6 kebab sticks
Baking paper

1 In a bowl, mix the ground beef, chopped parsley, egg, salt and pepper (1). Spread the mixture into a flat disk shape, then place a mini mozzarella ball in the middle and close the mixture around it to form a ball. Repeat until you have 6 balls.

2 Cut the ends off the onions, then remove the skin and carefully take off the outer layers, keeping them intact. Place the meatballs inside the onion rings (2) and wrap each one in 2 slices of bacon.

3 Place a kebab stick in the center of each ball and bake for 30 minutes at 350°F on the baking tray (3). After baking, dip the lollipops in barbecue sauce and serve (4).

 CHEFCLUB TIP
Does slicing onions make you teary? To avoid crying when cutting an onion, simply run it under the tap briefly beforehand. It's a little trickier to cut a wet onion, but at least you'll be able to see what you're doing!

TRIPLE THREAT CHEESE FONDUE

THE FONDUE TO END ALL FONDUES....IT'S GOING DOWN IN THE HISTORY BOOKS

 4 PEOPLE

 PREPARATION
35 minutes

 INGREDIENTS
1 large loaf of crusty bread
3x1 cup of your favorite
cheeses for melting
2 oz bacon
1 onion
1 tbsp grated parmesan
1 garlic clove
½ bunch of parsley
Dried rosemary
1 tbsp olive oil

 EQUIPMENT
1 baking tray
Baking paper

1 Cut 3 squares in the top of the loaf of bread, being careful not to cut through the bottom. Cut the removed bread squares into breadsticks (1).

2 Fill each of the squares with a different type of your chosen cheeses (2-4). Add a topping to each cheese; for example fried onions, dried rosemary, and grilled bacon (5-6). Repeat the cheese and topping layers and finish with a layer of cheese on the top of each square.

3 Combine the olive oil with finely chopped garlic, chopped parsley, and parmesan cheese. Place the loaf of bread and the breadsticks on the baking tray on top of baking paper, and brush the breadsticks with the olive oil mixture (7).

4 Bake for 30 minutes at 400°F (8). Serve hot by dipping the breadsticks into the melted cheese fondues (9).

 CHEFCLUB TIP
Contrary to what you might think, the softer and creamier cheeses don't necessarily contain the most calories – in fact, it's the opposite! Pressed and cooked hard cheeses contain very little water and therefore concentrate the fat. Bring on the Camembert!

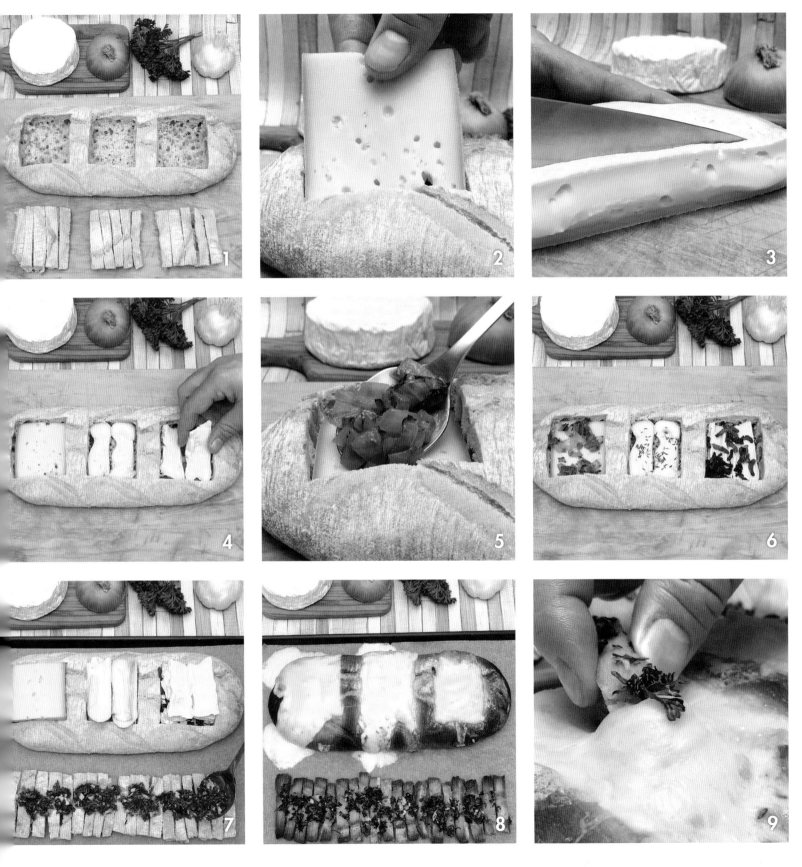

CURLY FRIES

MAKE THEM AS BIG AS YOU WANT!

 4 PEOPLE

 PREPARATION
35 minutes

 INGREDIENTS
3 large potatoes
⅓ cup butter
1 tsp salt
1 tsp sugar
⅔ cup water
¾ cup flour
3 eggs
2 cups vegetable oil

 EQUIPMENT
1 piping bag
1 piping nozzle
1 saucepan

1 Peel and cook the potatoes in salted boiling water, then drain (1) and mash them to get a smooth consistency.

2 In a saucepan, boil the butter, sugar, salt and water together. Remove the pan from the heat, add the flour and mix well.

3 Beat the eggs together and gradually add them to the dough mixture, mixing until the dough is smooth and thick (2).

4 Add the potato mash to the dough and place the whole mix in a piping bag. Pipe the mix in spirals straight into hot oil and cook until golden (3). Drain the fries on a paper towel to remove excess oil, and enjoy with your favorite dipping sauce (4).

 CHEFCLUB TIP
For this recipe, the type of piping nozzle you use will make all the difference as to how your fries will turn out. A star nozzle will give a star shape with crispier edges, but if you have no piping set simply use a freezer bag and cut a small corner off and pipe using that. Not as neat but will still taste delicious!

CANNELLONI BITES

A SPICY SURPRISE

 2 PEOPLE

 PREPARATION
40 minutes

 INGREDIENTS
*1 box (250 g) cannelloni
pasta
2 garlic cloves
1 ¼ cups chopped tomatoes
Red Tabasco® sauce
24 mini buffalo mozzarella
balls
1 ¼ cups flour
4 eggs
1 cup breadcrumbs
Parsley*

 EQUIPMENT
*1 Ziploc® freezer bag
1 baking tray
Baking paper*

1 Cook the cannelloni for 3 minutes in boiling salted water (1), then drain and cut each cannelloni in half.

2 In a frying pan, cook the chopped tomatoes, finely chopped garlic, chopped parsley and 5 (or more!) drops of Tabasco® for a few minutes (2), then place the sauce in a Ziploc® freezer bag.

3 Place the mini mozzarella balls on a plate and add a piece of cannelloni on top. Fill the tube with the sauce and enclose the tube by adding another mozzarella ball on top.

4 Dip the filled cannelloni in flour, then in beaten egg, and finally in breadcrumbs (3).

5 Place them on a baking tray lined with baking paper, and bake for 15 minutes at 375°F. Enjoy hot (4).

 CHEFCLUB TIP
You can choose what size you want these depending on the occasion! For smaller bite-size pieces you can use Rigatoni pasta tubes, or for larger ones you can use whole cannelloni without cutting them in half. You can even add ground beef to the sauce if you like!

FLOWER PETAL PIE

THEY LOVE YOU...THEY LOVE YOU NOT...WHO CARES WHEN THERE'S PIE!

 6 PEOPLE

 PREPARATION
60 minutes

 INGREDIENTS
3 sheets of puff pastry
1 ¼ cup ground beef
2 cups hard cheese
4 tbsp tomato paste
1 tbsp mustard
2 tbsp milk
Basil
Salt and pepper

 EQUIPMENT
1 large tart tin
1 cheese grater

1 Unroll the pastry, and using a glass, cut out as many circles of dough as possible, then remove the excess dough.

2 In a bowl, mix the ground beef, tomato paste, mustard, chopped basil leaves, salt and pepper using a fork (1). Grate half of the cheese. Place a spoonful of the beef mixture in the middle of half of the dough circles, and in the other half put a spoonful of the grated cheese. Fold each circle in half, then bring the two points together to form petals (2).

3 Arrange the petals in the tart tin, alternating between meat and cheese rings, to form one large flower. Add a small cube of cheese to the hollows between the dough petals (3).

4 Brush the dough petals with milk, then bake for 45 minutes at 350°F. Enjoy hot (4).

 **CHEFCLUB TIP**
To brown the pastry nicely as it bakes, there are different methods: use milk for just a light glaze, egg yolk for a bright and yellow finish, or olive oil for a nice taste. You can also use coffee grounds for sweet recipes!

PIZZA BITES

GET YOUR PIZZA FIX WHENEVER YOU NEED IT

 4 PEOPLE

 PREPARATION
35 minutes

 INGREDIENTS
2 ready-to-bake pizza
doughs
8 mini buffalo mozzarella
balls
1 salmon fillet
2 ½ tbsp crème fraîche
2 slices of prosciutto ham
⅓ cup grated cheese
½ cup feta
4 cherry tomatoes
Tomato sauce
Basil
Dill

 EQUIPMENT
1 ice cube tray
1 baking tray
Baking paper

1 Lay one pizza dough over the ice cube tray, then use your fingers to gently push the dough into each of the wells (1-2).

2 Place in each row the following ingredients (3-6):
– 1 mini mozzarella ball and 1 basil leaf
– ½ cherry tomato and a cube of feta cheese
– 1 piece of prosciutto ham and grated cheddar cheese
– 1 cube of salmon, crème fraîche and dill

3 Cover the ice cube tray with the second piece of pizza dough and use a rolling pin to seal the dough together, then remove the excess dough (7). Put the ice cube tray in the fridge for 10 minutes, then remove the pizza cubes and separate them with a knife.

4 Arrange the pizza cubes on the baking tray lined with baking paper (8), and bake for 20 minutes at 350°F. Serve with tomato sauce for dipping (9).

 CHEFCLUB TIP
This recipe is dedicated to anyone who loves appetizer bites! You can make the bites using your favorite ingredients, or even just use the leftovers in your fridge!

KING CROQUE

AN IDEAL APPETIZER

 8 PEOPLE

 PREPARATION
45 minutes

 INGREDIENTS
4 sheets puff pastry
4 slices of ham
3 cups grated Swiss cheese
2 cups bechamel sauce
1 egg yolk

 EQUIPMENT
1 springform pan

1 Unroll one sheet of puff pastry and place it in the springform pan. Place a slice of ham in the center, and pour the bechamel around the edge of the dough (1), then sprinkle grated cheese on top.

2 Repeat these steps three times and cover with the fourth sheet of puff pastry. With a knife, cut a star in the center of the dough and fold each point outwards to form a crown (2).

3 Brush the dough with egg yolk (3), then bake for 25 minutes at 400°F. Remove and enjoy warm with a side of salad (4).

 CHEFCLUB TIP
You can modify this recipe to make it vegetarian by replacing the ham with slices of zucchini. To do this, use 2 zucchinis and place 3 zucchini slices side by side where you would put a slice of ham.

ZUCCHINI FRITTERS

READY TO EAT IN JUST 5 MINUTES

 4 PEOPLE

 PREPARATION
15 minutes

 INGREDIENTS
3 zucchinis
3 large buffalo mozzarella balls
1 cup all-purpose flour
3 eggs
½ cup breadcrumbs
½ cup grated parmesan
1 quart vegetable oil
Tomato sauce

 EQUIPMENT
1 vegetable peeler
Toothpicks

1 Cut the zucchini into thin slices using a peeler, and cut the mozzarella into thin slices as well.

2 Place 2 slices of zucchini in an "X" shape over each other and put a slice of mozzarella in the middle (1). Fold the edges of the zucchini around the mozzarella and repeat the process to form as many zucchini bundles as possible (2).

3 Stick a toothpick into the center of each zucchini bundle (3). Coat them in flour, beaten egg, grated parmesan, and breadcrumbs.

4 Fry for 2 minutes in hot oil, then drain and remove the toothpicks. Serve warm with tomato sauce to dip (4).

 CHEFCLUB TIP
Don't know when your oil is hot enough? Don't panic, just throw a small piece of zucchini or stale bread in your oil, and if the color changes quickly the oil is ready!

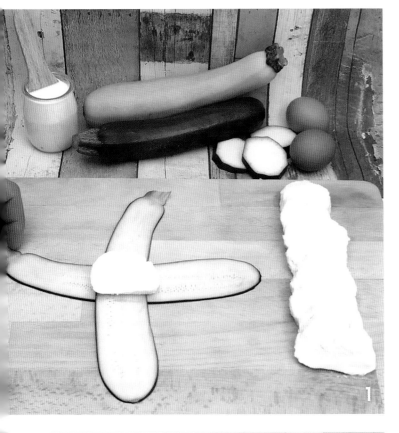

1

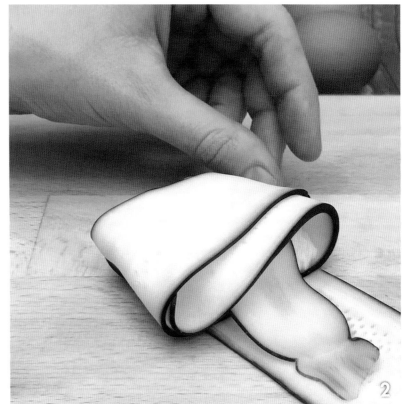

2

3

4

CRISPY OMELETTE

A SURPRISING ADDITION TO MAKE YOUR OMELETTE EVEN BETTER!

 6 PEOPLE

 PREPARATION
20 minutes

 INGREDIENTS
8 eggs
1 red pepper
1 green pepper
1 onion
1 large bag potato chips
Tomato sauce
Olive oil

 EQUIPMENT
1 large frying pan
1 ramekin

1 Crush the potato chips into small pieces, then beat the eggs in a bowl and stir in the crushed chips

2 Chop the onion and peppers into small pieces and fry them in a pan for about 10 minutes. Then add the vegetables to the egg & chip mixture (1).

3 Pour a drizzle of olive oil into a hot frying pan, and place an upturned ramekin dish in the center of the pan (2). Pour the egg mixture around the ramekin and cook for 3 minutes. Turn the omelette over with a large plate and put it back on the heat for 3 minutes (3).

4 Slide the omelette onto a plate and pour tomato sauce into the ramekin. Serve hold or cold by dipping the omelette pieces into the tomato sauce (4).

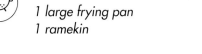 **CHEFCLUB TIP**
You can vary this recipe by choosing your favorite flavor of chips—sour cream and onion omelette, anyone?

FRIED CANNELLONI

IT'S APPETIZER TIME!

 4 PEOPLE

 PREPARATION
30 minutes

 INGREDIENTS
12 cannelloni
1 zucchini
9 oz ricotta
12 slices of coppa ham
1 ¼ cups flour
2 eggs
1 ⅔ cups breadcrumbs
1 quart vegetable oil
Tomato sauce

 EQUIPMENT
1 sauté pan or skillet with high sides
1 Ziploc® freezer bag

1 Cook the cannelloni for 3 minutes in salted boiling water. Drain and run them under cold water to stop them from cooking.

2 Cut the zucchini into sticks the same length as the cannelloni, then fill each cannelloni with one stick of zucchini.

3 Mix the ricotta, diced coppa ham, and chopped chives. Place the mixture into a Ziploc® freezer bag, close it, and cut the bottom corner to make a pastry bag. Fill the cannelloni with this mixture on both ends.

4 Cut the cannelloni in half and bread them by dipping first in the flour, then the eggs, and finally the breadcrumbs.

5 Fry them for 2 minutes in boiling oil until golden brown, then drain. Enjoy hot with tomato sauce.

 CHEFCLUB TIP
When cooking the cannelloni, you can also put them in a pot of covered boiling water and leave them until they're al dente!

EGGS-PLODING BAGUETTE

PERFECT FOR A WEEKEND BRUNCH

 3 PEOPLE

 PREPARATION
20 minutes

 INGREDIENTS
1 French baguette
2 tsp sunflower oil
6 eggs
3 ½ oz diced bacon
6 slices of edam
6 slices of cheddar
Chives

 EQUIPMENT
Plastic wrap
1 baking tray
Baking paper

1 Cut the baguette into pieces 2.5 inches in length (1). Form a hollow by pushing down on the inside of the bread.

2 Place plastic wrap over a bowl. Brush the plastic wrap with sunflower oil. Pour in an egg. Twist and knot the plastic wrap to seal it. Repeat this 5 times. Cook the eggs in boiling water for 4 minutes, then add one into each piece of bread (2).

3 Cook the diced bacon in a frying pan, then add them to the bread on top of the eggs. Add a slice of edam and a slice of cheddar on top (3).

4 Place under the grill for 5 minutes at 400°F. Sprinkle with chopped chives and serve (4).

 CHEFCLUB TIP
Eggs are a complete source of protein, as they contain all nine essential amino acids we need and cannot produce in our body ourselves. They also contain selenium, vitamin D, B6, B12 and minerals such as zinc, iron and copper. A perfect way to fuel your body for the day!

SPOON APPETIZERS

THESE SPOONS WON'T LAST LONG

 4 PEOPLE

 PREPARATION
30 minutes

 INGREDIENTS
For 8 spoons and 8 baskets:
1 sheet puff pastry
2.5 oz tuna
4.5 oz of ricotta
¼ cup tomato sauce
8 green olives
2 cherry tomatoes
8 basil leaves
Salt and pepper

  **EQUIPMENT**
8 teaspoons
1 baking tray
2 pieces of baking paper
1 water bottle cap

1 Arrange the spoons in a star shape on the puff pastry, then cut out the dough around the spoons (1). Using the bottlecap, cut out 8 small circles from the dough and use the rest of the puff pastry to make 8 small strips.

2 Place the spoon-shaped pieces (with the spoons still on top) and the circles on the baking tray, covered with one sheet of baking paper. Add tomato sauce and an olive to each circle, then cover them with a strip of pastry (2). Bake for 15 minutes at 400°F.

3 Mix the tuna and ricotta, then add salt and pepper. Make a cone with the second piece of baking paper and place the mixture into the cone.

4 Take the spoons out of the oven, then top them with the tuna and ricotta mixture using the baking paper as a pastry bag. Garnish each spoon with a slice of cherry tomato and a basil leaf (3) and enjoy (4).

> **CHEFCLUB TIP**
> Remember that moisture is puff pastry's worst enemy! For a nice and flaky finish, brush the pastry with egg white and put it in the oven for 5 minutes. It will be protected from moisture and keep its crisp texture!

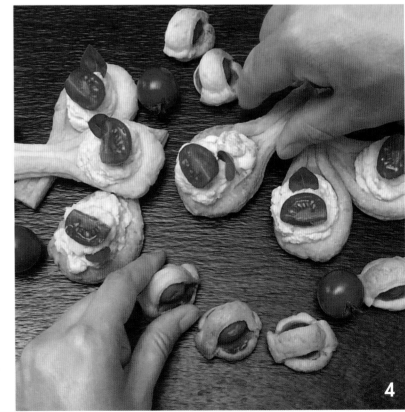

EASY CHEESY ONION RINGS

A QUICK AND DEPENDABLE FAVORITE

 6 PEOPLE

 PREPARATION
15 minutes

 INGREDIENTS
4 red onions
1 large buffalo mozzarella ball
1 ¼ cups flour
1 ⅔ cups breadcrumbs
4 eggs
2 cups vegetable oil
Tomato sauce

 EQUIPMENT
1 saucepan

1 Cut the onions into thick slices, then separate the rings with your fingers (1). Cut the mozzarella into long strips.

2 Take 2 onion rings of different sizes so you can fit pieces of the mozzarella between them (2). Repeat this process to make as many onion rings as possible then place them in the freezer for 1 hour.

3 Coat all the onion rings by dipping them into flour, then egg, and finally breadcrumbs (3). Fry for 5 minutes in hot oil. Serve hot and fresh with plenty of tomato sauce (4).

 CHEFCLUB TIP
For lovers of other kinds of cheese, you can replace the mozzarella with Camembert. Try and use a cheese with the same texture as the mozzarella so the onion rings are easy to assemble. You'll get melty, gourmet onion rings every time!

For those who make you swoon...

LOVE

OMELETTE TOAST

NEVER WORRY ABOUT YOUR OMELETTE TURNING INTO SCRAMBLED EGGS AGAIN!

 2 PEOPLE

 PREPARATION
15 minutes

 INGREDIENTS
4 slices of bread
½ red pepper
½ green pepper
2 slices of ham
4 eggs
⅔ cup grated mozzarella
Oil

 EQUIPMENT
1 frying pan
1 spatula

1 Using a knife, cut the middle out of the bread, leaving only the crust edge (1). Chop the peppers and the ham into small pieces.

2 In frying pan, cook the peppers and ham in oil. Push ¼ of the mix together to form the shape of the bread crust, then place the crust over the top around the ham and pepper mix (2).

3 Beat an egg and pour it over the ham and peppers in the middle of the bread. Sprinkle the grated mozzarella on top and cook for 3 minutes (3).

4 Place the middle of the bread on the cheese and using a spatula, flip the omelette over. Cook for 2 to 3 minutes on the other side. Repeat the process with the other 4 slices of bread and enjoy hot (4).

 CHEFCLUB TIP
You can use goat cheese instead of mozzarella for a stronger flavor that complements the egg. For this, cut the goat cheese into small pieces so it cooks easily and evenly.

DORITOS® CHICKEN

CRISPY, CRUNCHY, AND CRIMINALLY TASTY

 2 PEOPLE

 PREPARATION
35 minutes

 INGREDIENTS
For 2 chicken breasts:
1 bag of Doritos® chips
2 slices of cheddar cheese
2 chicken breasts
1 ¼ cups flour
2 eggs
Guacamole

 EQUIPMENT
1 baking tray
Baking paper

1 Crush the Doritos® chips into small pieces with a rolling pin, and pour them into a bowl (1).

2 Roll the cheese slices up tightly, then roll half a chicken breast around each piece of cheese (2).

3 Dip the chicken in flour, then egg, then coat in the crushed Doritos® (3). Bake in the oven at 350°F for 25 minutes on a baking tray lined with baking paper, and serve hot with guacamole for dipping (4).

 CHEFCLUB TIP
This is a great way to use up old chips that have gotten stale. In the oven they will crisp up again and give a nice crunchy coating. You can also swap the Doritos® flavor for your own favorite!

CAULIFLOWER GRILLED CHEESE

GET CREATIVE AND ADD YOUR OWN FILLINGS!

2 PEOPLE

PREPARATION
20 minutes

INGREDIENTS
For 2 sandwiches:
1 small head cauliflower
4 slices of ham
½ cup grated parmesan
1 ¼ cup grated Swiss cheese
3 eggs
Chives
1 tsp paprika
Olive oil
Salt and pepper

EQUIPMENT
1 frying pan
1 blender
1 spatula

1 Put the cauliflower in a blender and mix with the eggs, grated parmesan, chives, paprika, salt and pepper.

2 Spread this mixture in a pan with a drizzle of olive oil, forming 4 squares with the spatula. Cook slowly over a very low heat for at least 5 minutes on each side, flipping them very carefully.

3 Add the ham and the grated cheese onto one slice, then close the sandwich by putting one cauliflower slice on top of the cheese and ham on the other. Allow them to cook for a few minutes till the cheese is melted. Enjoy hot as a big grilled cheese, or cut into triangles.

CHEFCLUB TIP
It's essential to cook the cauliflower on a low heat so that it sticks together and doesn't dry out.

STUFFED GNOCCHI DONUTS

MAMMA MIA!

 2 PEOPLE

 PREPARATION
45 minutes

 INGREDIENTS
For 4 donuts:
4 large potatoes
4 cups flour
8 slices of bacon
1 large buffalo mozzarella ball
4 tbsp ricotta
1 egg yolk
1 small glass of milk
8 cherry tomatoes
2 tsp baking powder
1 tbsp salt
Basil
2 cups vegetable oil
Olive oil

 EQUIPMENT
1 skillet with high sides
1 rolling pin
Paper towels

1 Peel, cut and cook the potatoes in salted water. Then drain and mash them with the egg yolk, flour, milk, baking powder and salt. Mix until you get a smooth, dough-like consistency.

2 Place the dough on a floured surface (1) and roll it out with a rolling pin. Once rolled out, cut 4 rectangles that are 8"x3".

3 Place 2 bacon slices vertically on a cutting board, spaced apart. Place the first dough rectangle horizontally across the bacon, and place thin slices of cherry tomato and a layer of ricotta in the middle of the dough. Add a few basil leaves, sliced mozzarella and a drizzle of olive oil. Close the dough together and roll the bacon up around it, and fold it together to form a ring (2). Repeat the process to form 4 donuts.

4 Fry the donuts in hot oil (3) until they are golden brown. Remove the excess oil by allowing them to dry on paper towels, then enjoy hot (4).

 CHEFCLUB TIP
With any excess dough, make small balls and let them simmer in boiling water. When they float to the surface you've got homemade gnocchi!

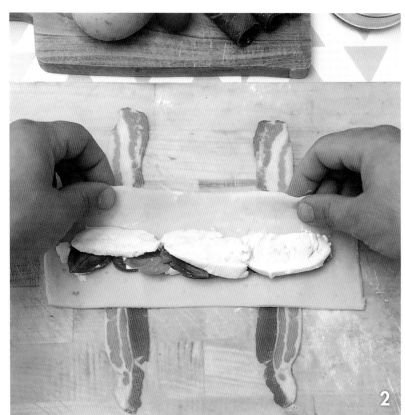

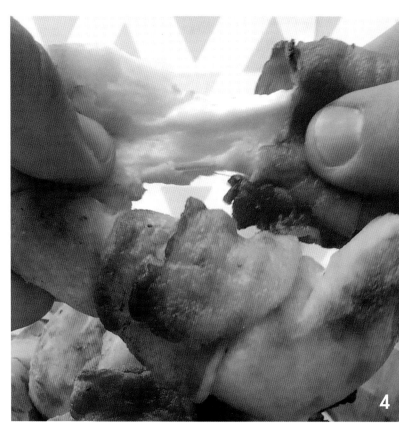

ONE-POT SPAGHETTI

A CHEESY, CREAMY DELIGHT

 2 PEOPLE

 PREPARATION
35 minutes

 INGREDIENTS
12 slices of bacon
1 large buffalo mozzarella ball
¾ cups Swiss cheese
¾ cups goat cheese
⅓ cup mascarpone
9 oz spaghetti (about half a box)
Chives
1 clove of garlic
Pepper
2 cups water

 EQUIPMENT
3 glasses
1 baking tray
Baking paper
Aluminum foil

1 On the baking tray covered with baking paper, place 3 glasses upside-down, then cover them with aluminum foil.

2 Arrange 2 slices of bacon in an "X" shape over each glass and cover the sides with the remaining slices (1-2). Bake for 15 minutes at 400°F, then allow them to cool before removing them from the glasses.

3 Cut the mozzarella into slices and cut the Swiss cheese into squares. Put them in a saucepan and add the mascarpone, spaghetti, and crushed garlic. Add pepper, then add water and allow the spaghetti to cook for the amount of time indicated, stirring occasionally (3).

4 Once the spaghetti is cooked, serve it in the bacon cups. Garnish with chives and enjoy hot (4).

 CHEFCLUB TIP
To peel garlic easily and end up with a beautiful, ready-to-use clove, grab a jar. Place your garlic in the jar, close it, then shake vigorously. Within a few moments, you'll notice that the skin has completely fallen off of the clove!

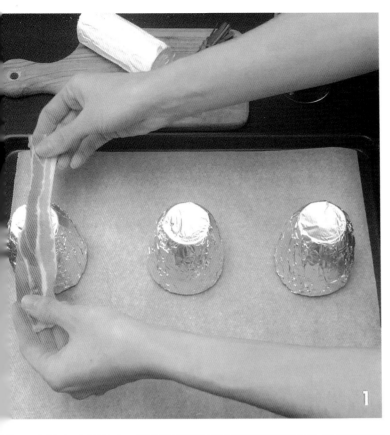

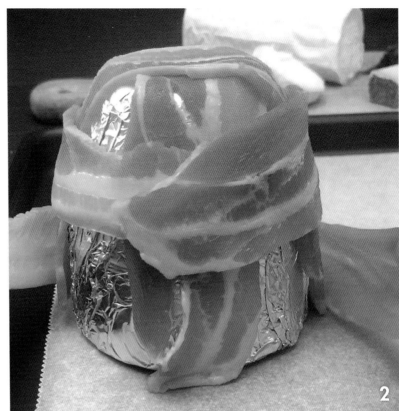

PIZZA BOATS

YOU CAN SAIL ALL THE WAY TO FOOD HEAVEN...

 2 PEOPLE

 PREPARATION
30 minutes

 INGREDIENTS
1 ready-to-bake pizza dough
1 cup ground beef
1 large buffalo mozzarella ball
12 sundried tomatoes
1 onion
2 garlic cloves
½ cup tomato sauce
1 egg
2 tbsp grated cheddar
Chives
Salt and pepper

 EQUIPMENT
1 baking tray
Baking paper

1 Cut the mozzarella and sundried tomatoes into pieces and place them around the edges of the pizza dough. Fold the edge of the pizza dough over them, then form 2 points at either end.

2 Finely chop the onion and garlic and mix them with the ground beef, tomato sauce, and salt and pepper and fill the middle of the dough with the mix. Sprinkle with the grated cheddar and break an egg in the middle.

3 Bake for 25 minutes at 350°F on a baking tray. Garnish with chopped chives and enjoy.

 CHEFCLUB TIP
If you want the egg to still have a runny yolk, add it to the pizza boat at the end of baking and let it cook for just 5 minutes. Guaranteed success!

MINI MOZZARELLA STICKS

SO GOOD YOU WON'T WANT TO SHARE....SHHHH!

 2 PEOPLE

 PREPARATION
20 minutes

 INGREDIENTS
3 large buffalo mozzarella balls
1 slice of prosciutto ham
1 sundried tomato
1 tsp ricotta
2 eggs
1 cup breadcrumbs
Basil
Oil
Ketchup

 EQUIPMENT
1 baking tray
1 rolling pin
1 frying pan

1 Grease an oven tray and place the 3 balls of mozzarella in the middle (1). Bake in the oven for 10 minutes at 350°F to melt the cheese. Remove the sheet of melted mozzarella and using a rolling pin, roll into a rectangle shape.

2 Cut the mozzarella sheet in half, and place the prosciutto ham and sundried tomato on one end of one half, and ricotta and basil leaves to the end of the other half. Roll the mozzarella up to form 2 sausage shapes (2).

3 Cut the rolled mozzarella into 1" pieces (3), and dip each piece in egg and then breadcrumbs and fry for 3 minutes in oil till golden brown all over. Enjoy hot dipped in ketchup (4).

 CHEFCLUB TIP
You can stuff the mozzarella sticks with any fillings you want, or even just leave them plain with mozzarella! We recommend creamy gorgonzola cheese, spicy jalepeños, or roasted red pepper. The possibilities are endless!

AVOCADO SURPRISE

EVERYTHING YOU NEED FOR A PERFECT BREAKFAST, ALL WRAPPED UP IN ONE

 2 PEOPLE

 PREPARATION
25 minutes

 INGREDIENTS
For 2 avocado surprises:
2 avocados
6 slices of bacon
2 eggs
¼ cup vegetable oil
Salt and pepper

 EQUIPMENT
Plastic wrap
2 ramekins
1 saucepan

1 Place a square of plastic wrap over each ramekin, then brush the inside with a drizzle of oil. Crack an egg into each ramekin and close the plastic wrap around the egg. Cook for 4 minutes in boiling water (1).

2 Cut the avocados in half and remove the skin, the pit, and some of the flesh to make room for the egg.

3 Remove the plastic wrap from the eggs and gently place them in the middle of the avocados (2). Place the other half of the avocados on top and wrap the whole avocado in 3 slices of bacon (3).

4 Fry the avocados in a pan for 10-12 minutes, turning frequently to cook all the bacon. Serve hot (4).

 **CHEFCLUB TIP**
You can also bake the bacon-wrapped avocados instead of frying them. Bake for around 15 minutes at 325°F for an equally beautiful result!

LINGUINE IN A PARMESAN BOWL

NO NEED TO WASH UP, JUST EAT THE DISHES TOO!

 2 PEOPLE

 PREPARATION
30 minutes

 INGREDIENTS
For 2 bowls:
11 oz linguine (about 2/3 of a box)
1 ½ cups grated parmesan
2 garlic cloves
¼ cup pine nuts
Cherry tomatoes
Basil
Olive oil
Salt and pepper

 EQUIPMENT
2 bowls
1 baking tray
Baking paper

1 Place baking paper on a baking sheet, then spread grated parmesan in 2 circles on top. Bake in the oven for 15 minutes at 350°F. Take them out of the oven and immediately place the soft parmesan disks on upturned bowls. As they cool they'll harden into the bowl shape.

2 Cook the linguine for 8 minutes in salted boiling water. Save a ladle full of the cooking water for later.

3 Fry the chopped garlic and pine nuts in a drizzle of olive oil. Add the cooked linguine, the ladle of cooking water, some fresh basil leaves and the grated parmesan, then mix it all together.

4 Fill the parmesan bowls with the linguine and garnish with cherry tomatoes, salt, and pepper. Enjoy!

 CHEFCLUB TIP
You can also make the parmesan bowls in the microwave instead. Place the grated parmesan circle on baking paper and cook for 45 seconds on full power!

THE SUSHI BURGER

A CULTURAL FUSION

 2 PEOPLE

 PREPARATION
30 minutes

 INGREDIENTS
For 2 sushi burgers:
1 cup sushi rice
3 tsp sugar
4 tsp rice wine vinegar
1 ¾ cups water
4 shrimps
1 fillet of salmon
1 avocado
½ cucumber
*1 sheet of nori seaweed
paper*
Soy sauce
Salt

 EQUIPMENT
1 plastic bottle
1 small bowl

1 Put the rice, sugar, vinegar, a pinch of salt, and water in a saucepan (1). Boil for 15 minutes until the rice is cooked.

2 Cut the salmon into small pieces, and slice the shrimp in half lengthwise. Cut the avocado and cucumber into thin slices (2).

3 Cut the top and bottom off of the plastic bottles to give you 2 plastic circle molds (3). Cut long strips from the seaweed sheet ½" wide (4).

4 Place 2 seaweed strips end to end, and add the plastic circle mold over the top (5). Add the cooked rice inside to give the base of the burger, then add a layer of chopped salmon, then avocado, then shrimp, then cucumber (6).

5 Remove the plastic mold, and use a small bowl to shape the top of the burger bun from the remaining cooked rice (7). Add the rice top then fold the seaweed strips over the top to hold it together (8). Serve with sesame seeds and soy sauce (9).

CHEFCLUB TIP
This meal is gluten free, so it's a great option for anyone with a restricted diet! Also, the healthy omega-3 fats and selenium in the salmon and avocado, as well as the iodine from the nori, are excellent nutrients for brain function. That makes this meal a "clever" choice!

ULTIMATE MASHED POTATO NESTS

OOZING WITH CHEESE, BACON, AND HAPPINESS!

 2 PEOPLE

 PREPARATION
50 minutes

 INGREDIENTS
For 4 nests:
2 large potatoes
4 ½ oz diced bacon
1 wheel camembert
1 egg
3 ½ tbsp butter
½ cup grated parmesan
Parsley
Salt and pepper

 EQUIPMENT
1 piping bag
1 piping tip
1 baking tray
Baking paper

1 Peel and cook the potatoes in boiling salted water, then mash the potatoes with egg, parsley, grated parmesan, butter, salt and pepper, and mix well to get a smooth consistency.

2 Fry the diced bacon in a pan until crispy, and cut the camembert into small chunks.

3 Place the mashed potato in the piping bag, and pipe small nests onto baking paper on a baking tray. Fill the nests with the bacon and camembert chunks.

4 Bake the nests for about 15 minutes at 350°F to get a crisp coat and melted cheesy middle. Enjoy hot and fresh.

 CHEFCLUB TIP
No piping bag? No problem! Use a freezer bag instead and just cut one of the corners off!

THE SUSHI BALL

WITH A HEART OF GOLD!

 2 PEOPLE

 PREPARATION
40 minutes

 INGREDIENTS
For 2 sushi balls:
1 cup sushi rice
4 slices of bacon
1 avocado
2 eggs
Pepper

 EQUIPMENT
2 bowls
1 baking tray
Baking paper
4 pieces of plastic wrap

1 Grill the bacon in the oven for 15 minutes at 325°F (1). Cook the sushi rice for 12 minutes in boiling water and boil the eggs for 4 minutes.

2 Form 2 circles out of the rice on plastic wrap sheets (2). Peel, pit and thinly slice the avocado (3) and arrange the slices in a flower shape on the rice (4).

3 Place a second sheet of plastic wrap over the avocado, then turn it over and place inside a bowl (5), then remove the top sheet of plastic wrap.

4 Sprinkle the chopped bacon over the rice, and place the eggs in the middle with a dash of pepper (6). Close the plastic wrap around the ball and twist to form 2 tight balls (7-8), then remove the plastic wrap. Serve fresh right away (9).

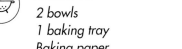 **CHEFCLUB TIP**
For this recipe, rinse the sushi rice in cold water before cooking. This gets rid of some of the starch, and it's still sticky enough after cooking to form perfect rice balls!

ITALIAN CROQUE-MONSIEUR

A FRENCH-INSPIRED ODE TO ITALY

2 PEOPLE

PREPARATION
30 minutes

INGREDIENTS
For 2 sandwiches:
4 slices of bread
4 slices of prosciutto ham
2 large buffalo mozzarella balls
¾ cups cream
¾ cups grated parmesan
3 eggs
1 ¼ cups 2% milk
1 cup all-purpose flour
Basil
Olive oil
Salt and pepper

EQUIPMENT
Plastic wrap
1 baking tray

1 Spread olive oil on each slice of bread, cut the mozzarella into slices, and place 2 mozzarella slices, 2 prosciutto ham slices, and 1 basil leaf on 2 of the slices of oiled bread. Add salt and pepper and close the sandwiches with the remaining bread slices.

2 Dip the sandwich in milk, then flour, then beaten eggs, and fry in a pan for a few minutes on each side over medium heat.

3 Cut 2 pieces of plastic wrap and place a sandwich on each piece, then close the plastic wrap and twist to form 2 balls. Let chill in the fridge for 10 minutes. Meanwhile, make a cheese sauce by heating cream and grated parmesan over low heat.

4 Take the sandwich balls out the fridge, remove the plastic wrap, and place them in an oven dish and bake for 15 minutes at 350°F. Serve the croque-monsieurs straight from the oven with the parmesan cream sauce. Enjoy!

CHEFCLUB TIP
For an egg-free recipe with a sweet spin, replace the eggs with honey instead. For example, mix a tablespoon of lavender honey with the milk and you'll get a sweet and savory mix instead. It's delicious!

FLOWER TARTS

EVERYONE WILL WANT A PIECE OF THIS BEAUTIFUL BUNCH!

 2 PEOPLE

 PREPARATION
15 minutes

 INGREDIENTS
1 pizza dough
4 hot dogs
4 eggs
⅔ cup grated mozzarella
Chives
Salt and pepper

 EQUIPMENT
4 kebab skewers
1 ramekin
1 toothpick
1 baking tray
Baking paper

1 Poke the kebab skewer through the hot dogs (1), and cut slices into them without cutting all the way through, and remove the end pieces. Take the skewers out and bend the hot dogs into circles.

2 Cut 4 circles out of the dough using a ramekin and place a hotdog on each one. Use a toothpick to fold the dough between the hot dog slices to make small flowers (2).

3 Add grated mozzarella to the middle of the flowers and season with salt and pepper, then bake for 10 minutes at 350°F on a baking tray.

4 Place an egg yolk in the middle of the flower and bake again for 3 minutes at 350°F (3). Garnish with chopped chives and enjoy with salad on the side (4).

 **CHEFCLUB TIP**
You can easily substitute the egg yolk with a mini-mozzarella ball for a creamy white center. Let your imagination run wild!

THE MAGIC SALAD

WATCH THIS SALAD DISAPPEAR

 2 PEOPLE

 PREPARATION
15 minutes

 INGREDIENTS
For 2 salads:
2 sheets of rice paper
16 shrimps
7 oz rice noodles
1 carrot
½ cucumber
½ lime
2 tbsp soy sauce
Sesame seeds
Peanuts
Fresh cilantro
¾ cup vegetable oil
Salt and pepper

 EQUIPMENT
1 large saucepan

1 Heat the vegetable oil in the saucepan, and fry the rice paper sheets one at a time to allow them to puff up.

2 Fry the shrimp and sesame seeds in a frying pan in a drizzle of vegetable oil. Meanwhile, leave the rice noodles to soak in boiling water and cut the carrot and cucumber into thin sticks.

3 Prepare the dressing by mixing the lime juice with the soy sauce and 1 tablespoon of vegetable oil.

4 Prepare the salad in the fried rice paper with the noodles, carrots, cucumber, and shrimp and cover in the dressing. Add some fresh cilantro, peanuts, salt and pepper, and enjoy.

 CHEFCLUB TIP
This recipe also works as a spring roll. Soak rice paper in hot water for a few seconds, then put it on a damp cloth to leave it soft. Divide the ingredients, and roll them up tightly into spring rolls, then enjoy!

One last bite for the road...

BONUS

M&M'S® PIE

CRUNCHY M&M'S® COMBINE WITH FRESH FRUIT FOR A COLORFUL DESSERT

 4 PEOPLE

 PREPARATION
40 minutes

 INGREDIENTS
1 piece pie dough
1 large bag of M&M's®
1 mango
2 kiwis
1 package of raspberries
1 package of blueberries
1 ¼ cups single cream
2 tbsp sugar
1 vanilla bean

 EQUIPMENT
1 pie plate
1 electric mixer
1 melon baller

1 Place the pie dough in the pie plate. Arrange M&M's® all around the edge of the dough (1), then fold the edges of the dough over them (2). Prick the bottom of the dough with a fork and bake for 20 minutes at 350°F. Remove from the oven and allow the dough to cool completely.

2 Cut the vanilla bean lengthwise and scrape out the inside using a the tip of a knife. Beat the cream, sugar, and vanilla together until smooth. Put it in the refrigerator to chill.

3 Scoop out balls of mango and kiwi using a melon baller (3). Rinse the raspberries and blueberries.

4 When the dough is cool enough, spread the whipped cream over the center of the pie, then cover each quarter with a different fruit. Finally, place yellow M&M's® over the mangoes, red M&M's® over the raspberries, green M&M's® over the kiwi, and blue M&M's® over the blueberries (4). Enjoy immediately.

 CHEFCLUB TIP
Don't throw out your empty vanilla pods! Place them in granulated sugar and you'll get delicious, vanilla-flavored sugar.

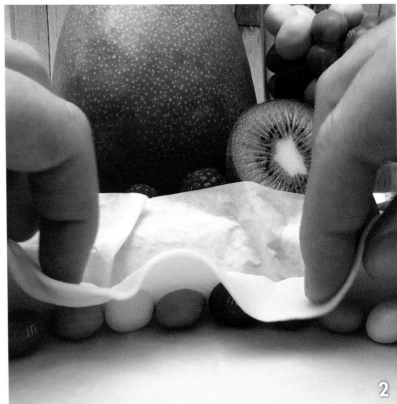

NUTELLA® AND BANANA CROWN

A GOLDEN CROWN OF DESSERT ROYALTY!

 4 PEOPLE

 PREPARATION
15 minutes

 INGREDIENTS
1 sheet of puff pastry
1 banana
6 tbsp Nutella®
3.5 oz milk chocolate
1 egg yolk

 EQUIPMENT
1 ramekin
1 pastry brush

1 Peel and slice the banana into pieces about ½" long, and arrange them on top of the puff pastry spaced slightly apart. Spread Nutella® over the banana slices (1).

2 Cut strips lengthwise, about ¾" wide, on the remaining pastry (2), then roll the dough up into itself. Join the 2 ends of the dough together to form a crown shape (3).

3 Brush the pastry with the egg yolk. Place a ramekin in the center of the crown and fill it with squares of milk chocolate.

4 Bake the crown for 30 minutes at 350°F (4). Enjoy by dipping pieces of crown into the melted chocolate.

 **CHEFCLUB TIP**
Don't throw away the banana peel, make a cake! Separate an egg into white and yolk, then whisk the egg white. Wash the banana peel with water and chop it up. In a bowl, mix the egg yolk with 1 ½ tbsp of butter, 3 tbsp of sugar, 1 scant cup of flour, 1 teaspoon of baking powder and the banana peel, then fold in the egg white. Bake for 20 minutes at 350°F and you'll get an unbeatable mini-cake, perfect for a breakfast treat!

THE BROOKIE

FOR WHEN YOU JUST CAN'T CHOOSE BETWEEN A BROWNIE AND A COOKIE...

 6 PEOPLE

 PREPARATION
60 minutes

 INGREDIENTS
2 ¾ cups flour
1 cup sugar
1 ¼ cups brown sugar
1 cup butter (2 sticks)
3 eggs
4 ½ oz dark chocolate
¼ cup chocolate chips
1 quart vanilla ice cream
⅔ cup pecan nuts
Caramel sauce

 EQUIPMENT
1 square baking tin
1 whisk

1 **Cookie dough:**
Whisk the brown sugar and one egg together until the mixture lightens in color (1) then add ½ cup of melted butter, 2 cups of seived flour, and the chocolate chips (2). Mix well to get a smooth dough. Leave for 15 minutes in the fridge to chill.

2 **Brownie dough base:**
Melt dark chocolate and ½ cup of butter (3) in a bowl over hot water. Stir in 2 eggs and add ¾ cup of sifted flour, the sugar, and the chopped pecans (4). Mix until smooth.

3 Grease the tin and pour in the brownie batter. Remove the cookie dough from the fridge and crumble it onto the top of the brownie dough (5-6). Bake for 30 minutes at 350°F then let the cake cool.

4 Remove the vanilla ice cream from the tub and use the tub to cut into the cake (7). Put some of the ice cream back in the box and spread it over the brookie (8). Enjoy with caramel sauce in your ready-made bowl!

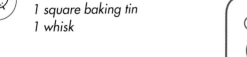

> **CHEFCLUB TIP**
> If you prepare the brownie batter and cookie dough in advance, you'll get an even better result! Store them in the fridge for 2 days to get a big cake that's crispy on the outside and soft and fluffy on the inside!

CHURRO ICE CREAM BOWLS

NO NEED TO BOTHER WITH THE DISHES, JUST EAT THE BOWL AS WELL!

 3 PEOPLE

 PREPARATION
25 minutes

 INGREDIENTS
For 6 churro bowls:
¼ cup butter
⅓ cup sugar
1 cup water
2 cups flour
2 eggs
2 cups vegetable oil
Cinnamon
Chocolate sauce
1 ball vanilla ice cream

 EQUIPMENT
1 muffin tin
1 piping bag
1 star piping nozzle
1 saucepan

1 In a saucepan over low heat, mix the butter, water, and half of the sugar then bring to a boil. Add the flour, then lower the heat again and mix (1).

2 Let the dough cool, then add the eggs and mix the dough well. Put the dough in a piping bag.

3 On an upside down muffin tin, pipe the dough over the muffin tin compartments (2). Place the tin in the freezer for 40 minutes until the dough is frozen together and can be removed from the tin intact (3).

4 Fry the dough in boiling oil for a few minutes until golden brown. Drain any excess oil on kitchen paper and roll the churro bowl in a mix of cinnamon and sugar.

5 Pour chocolate sauce into the churro bowl, then add a ball of vanilla ice cream. Drizzle more chocolate sauce on top and enjoy immediately (4).

> **CHEFCLUB TIP**
> You can use this trick to make savory versions too. Replace the churro dough with mashed potato instead, and use it as a bowl to hold gravy or your favorite sauce, perfect for dipping!

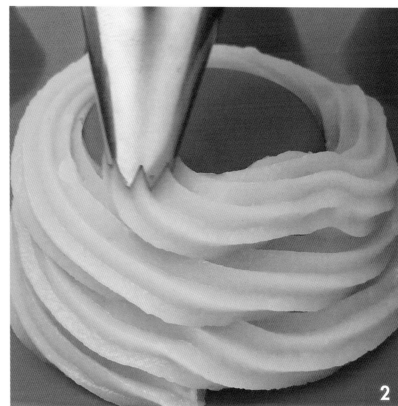

GIANT STUFFED COOKIE

IT'S IMPOSSIBLE TO RESIST THE MELTING CHOCOLATE MIDDLE...

 6 PEOPLE

 PREPARATION
40 minutes

 INGREDIENTS
1 cup butter (2 sticks)
1 cup brown sugar
3 cups flour
3 eggs
2 cups chocolate chips
12 Kinder® Maxi bars

 EQUIPMENT
1 round cake tin
1 baking tray
Baking paper

1 Mix the soft butter, flour, brown sugar, eggs, and chocolate chips together in a bowl (1).

2 On a lined baking tray, form a disk with half the cookie dough and place in the fridge for 30 minutes.

3 Grease the cake tin and spread the other half of the cookie dough inside the bottom and sides of the tin (2). Fill the inside with Kinder® chocolate bars arranged in a circle.

4 After chilling, use a plate on to cut a circle of dough the same size at the tin. Remove the excess dough.

5 Place the disk of cookie dough on top of the Kinder® chocolate (3) and bake for 25 minutes at 350°F. Remove the tin and enjoy warm (4).

 CHEFCLUB TIP
To make cutting and lifting the cookie dough easier, it must be allowed to chill in the fridge. If you feel it's too soft or may break, put it in the freezer for a few minutes and try again!

HONEY AND LEMON COCKTAIL

THIS HONEY AND LEMON SLUSHIE INCLUDES AN EXTRA KICK!

 3 PEOPLE

 PREPARATION
20 minutes

 INGREDIENTS
For 3 drinks:
3 lemons
7 oz prosecco
7 oz vodka
6 tbsp honey
Mint leaves

 EQUIPMENT
1 immersion blender
1 pitcher
1 ice cube tray
1 fine strainer
1 glass

1 Cut one end off of each lemon and remove the pulp from inside. Place the pulp in a strainer and squeeze all the juice out using the bottom of a glass. Save the empty lemons for serving.

2 Spread the lemon juice evenly into the ice-cube tray, filling them ⅔ full. Add the vodka, a few drops of honey, and a mint leaf into each compartment to fill the tray completely.

3 Place the ice cube tray in the freezer for 1 hour to form the lemon ice cubes. Place the whole lemons in the freezer as well.

4 Remove the ice cubes from the freezer and put them in a pitcher. Pour the prosecco into the jug and mix everything together to create a slushie. Pour the lemon vodka slush back into the lemons to serve. Cheers!

 CHEFCLUB TIP
Out of ice cubes? Here's a tip that could save you: use boiling water instead of cold water in your ice cube tray. Your ice will form a lot faster!

WHITE SANGRIA

FRESH, FRUITY, AND FESTIVE

 8 PEOPLE

 PREPARATION
20 minutes

 INGREDIENTS
1L Sprite®
1 bottle white wine
7 oz white rum
3 oranges
2 lemons
3 limes
3 peaches
2 cups strawberries
Mint leaves

 EQUIPMENT
2 glass mixing bowls
(1 large and 1 medium)
1 pitcher
1 roll of tape
Straws

1 Cut 1 orange, 2 lemons, and 2 limes into thin slices (1). Place the slices on the inside of the large bowl and add several mint leaves (2). Gently add water until the bowl is halfway full.

2 Place the second bowl inside the larger one (3) and tape them together (4-5). Store in the freezer for 12 hours until frozen, to make an ice punch bowl.

3 Remove the stems from the strawberries and cut them in half (6). Remove the pits from the peaches and cut them into quarters, then place the strawberries and peaches in the pitcher. Add the juice of the remaining two oranges, the juice of half a lime, and several mint leaves. Finally, pour the wine and rum into the pitcher (7).

4 Take the bowls out of the freezer, remove the tape, and gently remove the ice (8). Pour the sangria into the ice bowl and add Sprite® (9). Cheers!

 CHEFCLUB TIP
To easily remove the ice bowl from the mixing bowl, pour hot water into the smaller bowl and lift it out. Then, place the large bowl in hot water and you'll have no problem removing the ice bowl!

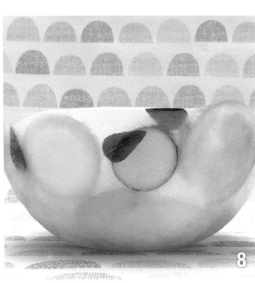

WHISKEY AND COKE SLUSHIE

TIME TO REINVENT THE CLASSIC FOR SUMMER

 6 PEOPLE

 PREPARATION
30 minutes

 INGREDIENTS
1.5L of Coca-Cola®
26 oz whiskey
1 lime
2 cherries
2 strawberries

 EQUIPMENT
1 blender
1 ice cube tray

1 Pour the Coca-Cola® into the ice cube tray and place it in the freezer for 3 hours (1).

2 Remove the frozen Coca-Cola® cubes from the freezer and put them in a blender with the whiskey. Blend together (2).

3 Pour the slushie mix into glasses and decorate with slices of lime, cherries and strawberries (3-4). Cheers!

 CHEFCLUB TIP
To make without a blender, mix only the juice of a lemon with the Coca-Cola® and place in an airtight container in the freezer until the liquid is completely frozen. To serve, take it out and scrape the surface with a fork to create a slushie. Divide between glasses and add whiskey before serving!

INDEX

THANK YOU AND MERCI!

We are a small team of 25 people in Paris, independent of any industrial group or corporation and your trust in us has allowed us to carefully curate this book with the same passion that we pour into our work everyday for Chefclub videos.

We chose Paris, the culinary capital of the world, to settle down, and we are very proud of the culinary diversity that our team brings: here, English, French, Japanese, Brazilian, Argentinian, Italian and Chinese foodies all come together.
We seek to explore cuisines from around the world and to learn from each others' experiences and differences.
Each country brings its passion and traditions and the US is no exception; it has served as an inspiration for several of the recipes you'll find in this book.

We hope you will have as much pleasure discovering this book as we have had making it.

The Chefclub team